TABLE

INTRODUCTION..................

QUIZ 1 3

QUIZ 2 5

QUIZ 3 7

QUIZ 4 9

QUIZ 5 11

QUIZ 6 13

QUIZ 7 15

QUIZ 8 17

QUIZ 9 19

QUIZ 10 21

QUIZ 11 23

QUIZ 12 25

QUIZ 13 27

QUIZ 14 29

QUIZ 15 31

Introduction

As a matter of fact, that humans living rhythm has been promoted immensely with the upgrading of neo-technology and hi-technology. However, reading books is still maintained as a healthy habit and it always proves its indispensable roles in our modern life. Reading books regularly is believed to keep our brains healthy, refresh our soul and slip away all stress at school, work, in our personal relationship or other issues faced in daily life. Books strongly support our analytical thinking skills and open up our imagination by diverse sources of information. Having thorough knowledge of different fields will help us to form the basis to overcome all obstacles and challenges in the future.

During pre-teen years, children are transitioning into secondary education and their lives inevitably become busier with homework, clubs, sports, and extra-curricular activities. This is also a time in which children are seeking greater independence. The main purpose of this book is to bring us more enjoyment as a family by asking one another mind-boggling riddles, that are a whole heap of fun. We believe it's really important to set quality time aside to stretch the mind and imagination and build bonds as a family.

As parents, we've found that through fun riddles our children have learned many educational and life-skills without realizing that this crucial learning is taking place. Three of the top skills that we believe riddles promote and encourage are the following:

1. The Ability to Think Outside the Box: Riddles help children apply logic and creativity to reach a conclusion. Children can learn literal and non-literal meanings of words. Children can learn to use their imaginations and become more inventive.

2. Problem Solving: In order to solve problems, children need to be able to find solutions, resolve issues, and develop creative options.

3. Enhancing Vocabulary: Unfamiliar words present parents with the perfect opportunity to encourage kids to use a dictionary. Parents can then encourage them to use the words in sentences to ensure that they understand their meaning. The riddles will certainly help to place new words in context in a fun way.

We hope you and your family has as much fun working through these riddles as our family did. Best luck!

QUIZ 1

1. A man got a $15 haircut. Using a $20 bill, he paid the barber but the barber had no change. The barber went to the flower shop and converted the $20 bill for a $10-dollar bill and two $5 bills. He gave $5 to the man for his change. The lady confronted the barber later, and told him that the $20 bill he gave her was falsified. The barber agreed, and gives another $20 bill to the lady. He tries to figure out how much money he'd lost later that day. How much did he lose?
2. What number gives the same answer when it is added to one and a half and when it is multiplied by the same number that is given?
3. What goes up, but never goes down?
4. It was brought to life by using electricity. It is made up of different body parts with bolts in the neck and its skin yellow. What is it?
5. It always fly, but goes nowhere. What is it?
6. You look away and pretend you don't know me when you release me, maybe because I always send your friends away. What am I?
7. How many days in a week begin with the letter "T"?
8. No one wants to sleep here. When you finally get to lay there, then it means you have left everything you loved behind. Once the lid is closed, that is the end of you, and you are buried for good. What is it?
9. I can be a drug and a lead in a story. What am I?
10. This can make ten octopuses laugh. What is it? Ten tickles. (Sounds like "tentacles.")

ANSWERS QUIZ 1

1. He lost 5$ and gave a free haircut, since the lady gave him $20, but got 20$ back and the man who earned the haircut gave the barber no money, but earned $5.
2. 3
3. Rain
4. Frankenstein's monster
5. Flag
6. Fart
7. Tuesday, Thursday, Today, and Tomorrow.
8. A coffin
9. Heroine
10. Ten Tickles (sounds like "tentacles")

QUIZ 2

1. When you're asked this question, you can't honestly answer with a yes. What is it?
2. How much dirt is there in a hole that is one-foot-deep, one-foot-long and one-foot-wide?
3. I am old, with tissues around me. Kids find me funny, but I've been long dead. Older people find me precious. What am I?
4. Jasmine fell off a long staircase. However, she was not hurt when she got up. How is that possible? Answer: She fell off the last stair.
5. I am the boss of the flock because I am big, tall and very strong. I can also run very fast. I have wings as well but sadly, I cannot fly. Who am I?
6. Why did the mummy never make any friends?
7. For one, it's insufficient. For two, it's perfect. For three, it's worthless. What is it?
8. What smells the most in the kitchen?
9. I can make you cry; make the dead live and form you smile, I can relive the past and reverse time. I form in a single second, but I last a life time. What am I?
10. Why did the student eat his homework?

ANSWERS QUIZ 2

1. Are you asleep?
2. None, or it wouldn't be a whole
3. A mummy
4. She fell off the last stair.
5. Ostrich
6. She was too wrapped in herself
7. A secret.
8. Nose
9. Memory
10. Because the teacher told him, it was a piece of cake.

QUIZ 3

1. During the day of his execution, a power outage occurs, and the prisoner in question is led to a room where he will live his last moments. He's been given the opportunity to choose the method of execution. He is shown an electric chair and a crocodile. Which method does the man have to choose to survive?
2. What is put on a table, cut, but never eaten?
3. It has a jacket without pants. What is it?
4. I help old people, I have a name of a bird, and I feed cargos on ships. I am not alive. What am I?
5. Mike is a butcher. He is really big. He's 7 feet tall, wears really big boots, and he has a big, bushy beard. What does he weigh?
6. I can save a memory forever, but fire can end my life. I've been around for a while, but I probably won't go out of style. What am I?
7. I am crushed, I am thrashed, I am clogged and I am also given or kept. Whatever I go through, I always remain the same, I am always whole.
8. A night watchman, while on patrol at night, dreams that the king will die in a plane crash due to the love he has for the king he quickly tells him in the morning, but the king tells him to not worry. He flies away and when he returns from the trip, he fires the night watchman. Why does the king fire the night watchman?
9. What's the favorite mode of transportation of rabbits?
10. What is pronounced as one letter, written with three, and is the same forwards and backwards? Eye

ANSWERS QUIZ 3

1. Electric chair, since there is no electricity, he won't be executed.
2. Deck
3. Book
4. Crane
5. Meat! Mike is a butcher so he weighs meat.
6. A picture
7. A heart
8. Because he knew that the watchman was sleeping during his duty, that's why he had dreams.
9. The hare-plane.
10. Eye

QUIZ 4

1. What type of house weighs the least?
2. How do you know that birthdays are good for you?
3. While two twins are in the room together with a King and Queen, there weren't any adults there. Why?
4. I am an animal. I die when I give birth to my offspring. What am I?
5. What word has twenty six letters?
6. What is the number that five is more than 1/5 of 1/10 of 1/4 of a thousand?
7. A man is sitting in his cabin. Hours after he gets out of his cabin and was already in a whole new place. How is this possible?
8. What grows when fed but dies when watered? Fire
9. Which is cheaper: bringing your Mother twice to the same movie or bringing 2 friends once to a movie?
10. What is it that has a bottom at the top of them?

ANSWERS QUIZ 4

1. A lighthouse
2. The more birthdays you have, the longer you live
3. All of them are beds.
4. Mayflies
5. Alphabet
6. 10 (1000÷4=250÷10=25÷5=5+5=10).
7. He is a pilot and airplanes have cabins
8. Fire
9. Bringing 2 friends to a movie once, because you'll only pay for 3 people while bringing your Mom twice to a movie will make you pay for 4 people.
10. Your legs

QUIZ 5

1. What needs to be taken from you before you have it?
2. You can see it somewhere in the middle of March and April that can never be seen either in the beginning nor ending of any month.
3. What is often returned, but never borrowed?
4. I can't go in no direction other than up and down. I am stuck, moving in a building. What am I?
5. What is flat, usually square, and made from trees but isn't wood?
6. There are several chickens and rabbits in a cage and they were the only ones. The heads were seventy-two while the feet counted two hundred. Try to use these numbers to know how many chickens and rabbits were there.
7. If an orange costs 18¢, while a pineapple costs 27¢, and a grape costs 15¢. With the same process, how much does the mango cost?
8. What goes up and down without moving?
9. You can neither see nor touch me. You cannot even feel me, but I can cook a meal for you. What am I?
10. I'm the beginning of eternity and at the end of time and space. I am the beginning of every end, and I am the end of every place. What am I?

ANSWERS QUIZ 5

1. Picture
2. The letter R.
3. Thanks
4. Elevator
5. Paper
6. Let r = the number of rabbits and c = the number of chickens. Then, r + c = 72. 4r + 2c = 200. To solve, we multiply the first equation by 2, and then subtract it from the second equation. 4r + 2c = 200 (-) r + 2c = 144 thus 2r = 56 r = 28 c = 44; so, there are 28 rabbits and 44 chickens.
7. 15¢. The cost is equal to 3¢ for each letter in the fruit's name.
8. Stairs
9. A microwave particle.
10. The letter E

QUIZ 6

1. Nightly they come without being fetched, what are they?
2. Are you good in math? If so, what is the ratio of a Jack O'lantern's circumference to its diameter?
3. Why couldn't Goldilocks sleep?
4. A cook's sister died, but the woman who died had no sister. How is that possible? Answer: The cook must have been her brother!
5. The blue house is beside the blueberry patch, the red house is beside the strawberry fields, and the yellow house is beside the banana trees. Where is the white house? Washington D.C
6. In the ground it's nothing, but give it time and it'll be something. What is it?
7. While on my way to St. Ives, I saw a man with his wife. They had seven children and each one had a cat. Each cat had a kitten and each kitten was in a sack. How many people were going to St. Ives?
8. A cloud was my mother, but I didn't stay with her for very long. The wind is my father, but he pushed us away. My son is the cool stream, and he is the reason I exist. I fall once in my life before I sleep in the earth one last time. What am I?
9. How can you place a pencil on the floor of a room so that no one can jump over it?
10. Most girls cannot go out without it. It makes them feel more beautiful. It is something that you apply on your body, lips and face.

ANSWERS QUIZ 6

1. Stars
2. It is a pumpkin pie!
3. Because of night-bears.
4. The cook must have been her brother!
5. Washington D.C
6. Seed
7. Just me. I was the only one going to St. Ives
8. Rain
9. You can put it next to the wall.
10. Make-up

QUIZ 7

1. I devour everything and people never think I'm dangerous, what am I?
2. What in the world can be half of an elephant?
3. Five people were on their way to a church. When it started to rain, 4 of the 5 ran for cover leaving the 5th one behind. And yet, the 4 who ran for cover got wet as they ran for cover while the man who got left behind stayed dry. How'd that happen?
4. What will you find at the end of a rainbow?
5. They live in houses as pets. It is said that they have more lives than any other creature. They are fluffy and sometimes want to be cuddled, while other times they just want to be left alone. They can be super active or super lazy. What are they?
6. He is very huge, has a big scar on his head, green, and likes to trick and scare away all the children when it is Halloween day. Who is he?
7. A book with one page, you read through a whole year, what am I?
8. What is never eaten before lunch?
9. What has a head, but can't think and has no limbs but can drive?
10. When a dog catcher catches 20 dogs in a week, how does he get paid?

ANSWERS QUIZ 7

1. Time
2. "ELEP" and "HANT"
3. The 5th person was in a coffin and the 4 other people were the pallbearers.
4. The end of the rainbow.
5. A cat
6. Prank-kenstien
7. Calendar
8. Dinner
9. Hammer
10. By the pound

QUIZ 8

1. What would you say if you met a ghost in your bedroom?
2. I always stay in the corner as I travel around the world. What am I?
3. Ghosts have a favorite spot on the road that they always want to travel at. Which is it?
4. He is very old, has a long white beard, and gives out the best presents. But, on Halloween day we all forget him. Who is he?
5. It is a very common little bug. However, even though it is so small, most people fear it so much. There is a name for this fear. It is called arachnophobia. Who is this little guy?
6. Abigail took an exam that had twenty questions. The total grade was calculated by giving ten points for every correct answer and deducting five points for each wrong answer. Abigail answered all twenty questions and earned a remark of 125. Solve how many wrong answers she had.
7. What 4-letter hour of the day is spelled the same forwards and backwards?
8. I always tell the truth even if I don't say and hear anything. What am I?
9. How many birthdays does the average kid have?
10. What is it that makes tears without sorrow? And takes its journey to heaven?

ANSWERS QUIZ 8

1. Hi Boo?
2. Stamp
3. The dead-end
4. Santa Claus
5. A spider
6. If Abigail got perfect score, she would have earned 200. Since she only scored 125, there is the missing 75 points. Each incorrect answer means losing a total of 15 points (10 for not having the correct answer and 5 for answering incorrectly) 75 divided by 15 is 5.
7. Noon
8. A mirror.
9. One.
10. Smoke

QUIZ 9

1. During what month people sleep the least?
2. I am something I like to live in a wardrobe. What am I?
3. What can go through towns and over hills without moving? Road
4. I can move quickly, but I have no legs. My skin will shed, but I stay the same. I can sound like bacon frying and I am hatched from an egg. What am I?
5. Hi, I'm Rodney and I live on a farm. With me on the farm are 4 other dogs Brownie, Spottie, Whitey, and Blackie. Who is the fifth dog on the farm?
6. I am the favorite drink down south. With just three (3) letters in my name, I can lose the last two and still sound the same
7. Forward I am heavy, but backwards I am not. What am I?
8. What goes further the slower it goes?
9. What gets harder to catch the faster you run?
10. It takes six wolves to catch 6 lambs within six minutes. So, how many wolves will be needed to catch 60 lambs in 60 minutes?

ANSWERS QUIZ 9

1. February, there are only 28/29 days
2. Clothes
3. Road
4. A snake
5. Me, Rodney.
6. Tea
7. Ton
8. Money
9. Breath
10. It takes 6 wolves. One wolf takes 6 minutes to catch a lamb. So, one wolf can catch 10 lambs in 60 minutes.

QUIZ 10

1. There are 3 stoves in front of you and you only have 1 match. The first stove is made of glass. The second stove is made of wood and the third stove is made of bricks. Which do you light up first?
2. A farmer hires some help to carry grain to his barn. The farmer carried one sack of grain to the barn while his helper carried only two sacks. Who did the most work? Read the sentence carefully before you answer.
3. If it takes three lions to catch three antelopes in three minutes, how many minutes does it takes 99 lions to catch 99 antelopes?
4. As you make your way across a bridge, you spot a boat full of people. And yet, there isn't even a single person on that boat. How can that be?
5. Which of the football team's players wears the largest helmet?
6. How do dog catchers get paid?
7. How many letters does the Greek alphabet contain?
8. More of me is hidden than is seen and I am lighter from where I came from. What am I?
9. What can point in every direction but cannot reach any destination by itself?
10. Sometimes I tend to shine, at times I am dull, I can be big, and I can be small. I can be pointy as well as curved. But don't ask me any questions because I am not smart enough to answer you even if I am sharp. So, what am I?

ANSWERS QUIZ 10

1. You light the match first.
2. The farmer did the most work. He carried a sack of grain while the helper just carried two sacks. They were empty.
3. Three minutes.
4. The boat was filled with married people and hence, there were no single people there.
5. The player with the largest head
6. By the pound.
7. 16. The (3) Greek (5) alphabet (8) equals 16 letters.
8. Iceberg
9. The compass
10. A knife.

QUIZ 11

1. Bamtaramushkabalurzeekhanz...how do you spell it?
2. I am always there in a distance, between the sky and the land. If you move closer to me, I still am distant. What am I?
3. What can be measured but not seen?
4. I have plenty of keys but don't have any doors, I have space but there are no rooms, I allow you to enter, but you can never leave. What am I?
5. A spider has $28 with it; an ant has $21 while the chicken has $7 with it. How much money will a dog have?
6. What becomes wetter and wetter even after it dries?
7. It is able to speak because it has a hard gone. You know what it is as soon as it has sung. What is it?
8. What is the word that even in plain sight remains hidden?
9. How did the tiger feel after eating Ellen De Generes and Jimmy Kimmel?
10. What is the four-digit number, without zeros, while the first and fourth digits are similar numbers, half of the sum of the second and the fourth digit is the second number, while the last digit is half of the sum of the first and the third numbers, consider that the sum of all digits is 24?

ANSWERS QUIZ 11

1. I and T ("it").
2. Horizon
3. Time
4. Keyboard.
5. $14 ($3.50 per leg).
6. A towel
7. Bell
8. Hidden
9. Funny
10. 6,666

QUIZ 12

1. What has hands, but cannot clap?
2. If strawberry jam has jelly, you have family, and a pencil has a paper, what do skeletons have?
3. Who is always the hottest person at all the Halloween parties?
4. I can be found on the internet or the newspaper or even a calendar. I can be rather expensive, but can also be cheap and affordable. I can be a treat for someone special. You can have me in the park, a movie theatre or even a restaurant. However, you have to be two to enjoy me. Who am I?
5. What has a tail and a head but does not have a body?
6. You put me in the soil to keep me alive and dig me up when I wither. What am I?
7. How far can a dog run into the woods?
8. Name all the numbers from 1 - 100, which have the letter "A" in their spelling.
9. Black cats are said to be bad luck. But, when is the one time you are guaranteed of bad luck when you cross the black cat?
10. A man shaves several times a day, yet he still has a beard. How is this possible?

ANSWERS QUIZ 12

1. Clock
2. No-body
3. The devil
4. A date
5. A coin
6. Plant
7. The dog can run into the woods only halfway.
8. None
9. When you are a mouse
10. He is a barber

QUIZ 13

1. It is a popular place, but no one ever wants to be there. Woe unto you if you are stuck there. It is full of many scary ghosts. Where is this place?
2. I am something I state the correct time perfectly twice a day- What am I?
3. You can hear me, but you can never touch nor see me. What am I?
4. Besides Winnie the Pooh, what else wears a jacket with no pants?
5. What can travel the whole way around the world while staying in the very same corner?
6. What is that over the head and under the hat?
7. Kevin flew to Australia at the fantastic speed of a thousand miles per hour. He picked up his friend and flew back, the extra weight caused the plane to only fly 500 miles per hour. What is Kevin's average speed?
8. I am a figure of speech, but I don't say the truth- What am I?
9. What number has all letters in alphabetical order when spelled out?
10. What never gets any wetter than it is today, no matter how hard it rains?

ANSWERS QUIZ 13

1. The haunted house
2. Stopped Time
3. Voice
4. A book.
5. A postage stamp
6. Hair
7. Kevin flew at 666.67 miles per hour over his entire trip.
8. Irony
9. Forty
10. The ocean or lake

QUIZ 14

1. I hate the rain and people hate me just as much because they believe that I am bad luck. What am I?
2. You pump it, but it is not a tire. It is a fluid and a vampire's all-time meal. What is it?
3. At times it is hot, other times it is either sweet or better. Some people love it when it is given to them as a gift. It comes in different shapes of blocks, chips and bars. Other times it is just a fountain that you can dip. What is it?
4. I am not alive, but I have five fingers. What am I?
5. I am a flying creature and very colorful, but no, I am not a rainbow. I am a very social creature and I know I am very beautiful, but I am not a human being. Who am I?
6. John and Peter were running a 100-meter race. After the first race, John beats Peter by 5 meters. To be fair, the next round is that John stood 5 meters behind the starting point. If the both of them ran at the same speed, who will win the second race?
7. Two fathers and sons walk into a store. They each buy biscuit worth of $50, but they all spend $150 in total. How is that possible?
8. There were five soccer teams that were competing and they have to face each other only once. The teams had 2 points each for a win and after the tournament, here is the point table: Manchester UTD was 6, Barcelona was 5, Bayern was 4, Milan was 2, and Real Madrid was unknown. How many points did Real Madrid end up with?
9. How can you create a fire using only 1 piece of stick?
10. We are flowers, but not ordinary flowers. We can French kiss and even smooch. What kind of flowers are we?

ANSWERS QUIZ 14

1. A black cat
2. Blood
3. Chocolates
4. A glove
5. Butterfly
6. John wins again. In the first race John ran 100 meters in the time it took Peter to run 95 meters. So in the second race when Peter is at the 95-meter mark John will also be there (since 100 - 5 = 95). Since John is faster he will pass Peter in the last 5 meters of the race.
7. They are three, the grandfather, the father, and the son.
8. There is a total of ten matches. Tw points were distributed to the winning. Therefore 10 x 2 = 20 points is the sum of all the teams' points. 6 + 5 + 4 + 2 +? =20,? = 3
9. By using a matchstick.
10. Tulip flowers

QUIZ 15

1. I am object you use which is 6 letters-word, but if you remove the first letter and replace it with "c" people hate it- What am I?
2. I always answer to your call, but I can be inaudible. What am I?
3. Dexter was 25 years old 2 days ago. Next year, he will be 28 years old. How can this be?
4. What is the name given to a funny skeleton that makes you giggle and laugh?
5. What can you always count on?
6. Which cheese is made backward?
7. What did the terrible spider say to the poor fly on Halloween?
8. I have six letters, remove one letter, and there are only twelve that remains. What am I?
9. What word stars with IS, with the ending AND, and has LA in the center?
10. Imagine that you are in a ferry boat located in the middle of the Caspian Sea. Suddenly, your boat becomes surrounded by two whales and a shark. They're circling your boat and are about to eat you alive! What are you going to do to stop this? Answer: You should stop imagining!

ANSWERS QUIZ 15

1. Basket (replace the first letter with C, it's casket)
2. Echo
3. Today is January 1. Two days ago was December 30, and his 26th birthday was yesterday, December 30. On December 30 this year, he turns 27 and next year, he turns 28 on December 30.
4. A funny bone
5. Fingers
6. Edam
7. The web is the trick and you are obviously the treat
8. Dozens
9. Island
10. You should stop imagining.

Printed in the USA
CPSIA information can be obtained
at www.ICGtesting.com
LVHW021614261124
797692LV00008B/630